COMING TO
GOD

SADLIER'S
New Edition
Coming to Faith Program

FAITH ALIVE
AT HOME AND IN THE PARISH

Dr. Gerard F. Baumbach

Dr. Eleanor Ann Brownell

Moya Gullage

Joan B. Collins

Helen Hemmer, I. H. M.

Gloria Hutchinson

Dr. Norman F. Josaitis

Rev. Michael J. Lanning, O. F. M.

Dr. Marie Murphy

Karen Ryan

Joseph F. Sweeney

Patricia Andrews

with

Dr. Thomas H. Groome
Boston College

Official Theological Consultant
   Rev. Edward K. Braxton, Ph. D., S. T. D.

Scriptural Consultant
   Rev. Donald Senior, C. P., Ph. D., S. T. D.

Catechetical and Liturgical Consultants
   Dr. Gerard F. Baumbach
   Dr. Eleanor Ann Brownell

Pastoral Consultants
   Rev. Msgr. John F. Barry
   Rev. Virgilio P. Elizondo, Ph.D., S. T. D.

William H. Sadlier, Inc.
9 Pine Street
New York, New York 10005-1002

Dear Family,

The Sadlier family has designed **For the Family:** *Faith Alive at Home and in the Parish* especially for you! Here are some of its exciting features.

The **Family Faith Background** helps you become familiar with what your child is learning. It also offers a family prayer or activity for you to share with your child.

Activities and Prayer Experiences enables you to share songs, Scripture stories, prayer experiences, and liturgical activities with your child at home and in your parish.

Faith Summary: Learn by Heart Learn by heart summarizes the doctrinal content of each section.

Review helps you to discern your child's understanding of the faith content and message. **Stickers** for Grades 1–3 are provided to place on the page when the work is completed. The answers for the questions are found at the end of the booklet.

Family Scripture Moment provides an easy-to-use way to use the Bible to listen to and to pray over God's word. The simple study and reflection approach of this section can strengthen your family's love for the Scriptures and help you to apply scriptural teaching to daily life.

Finally, you can remove **My Catholic Faith Book** (Grades 1–3) for family use in reviewing Catholic teaching with your child. Each of these sections follows the four-part structure of the Catechism of the Catholic Church: Creed, Sacraments, Morality, Prayer.

We encourage you to do as many of these activities as you can with your child. In today's busy world it is so important to spend time together as a family—talking, listening, caring for, and praying with one another. At the Last Supper Jesus prayed,"… May they all be one." (John 17:21) It is our sincere hope and prayer that you and your family grow in love and unity.

All of Us in the Sadlier Family

In this opening lesson your child was welcomed to first grade, both as an individual and as a member of a group. It is important that children feel part of a Christian community, especially your parish community, as they begin to explore together what it means to belong to the family of God.

This year your child's program in learning about our Catholic faith is called *Coming to God*. You have already spent time preparing your child for this continuing growth of coming to God, even without thinking about it. You have, informally and gently, been teaching your child about God and about God's love all along. It will be important that you continue to take an even more active role in guiding your child's growth in faith. Here are some ways the *Coming to God* program might assist you.

■ Talk about each lesson together, including the pictures and artwork, if possible, since they are an essential part of the program. Encourage a conversation about the *Faith Summary* statements. The symbol reminds you to help your child learn these by heart. You might ask a question for each statement.

■ Invite your child to share with you any songs, poems, or experiences of prayer that have been learned or shared. Even before truths of our Catholic faith are fully understood, they can be absorbed through a favorite song or prayer.

■ Use the *Faith Alive at Home and in the Parish* pages (this is the first of them) to continue and to expand your child's catechesis through the experience of the community of faith in your family and in the parish family. There will be a variety of activities on these pages. Try to do at least one with your child.

Family Scripture Moment is offered as a unique opportunity for the family to share faith by "breaking open" God's word together. The "moment" can be as brief or as long as you wish. A simple outline is suggested as one way to use this time together.

■ **Gather** together as a family. All can participate from the youngest to the oldest.

■ **Listen** to God's word as it is read, slowly and expressively, by a family member.

■ **Share** what you hear from the reading that touches your own life. Give time for each one to do this.

■ **Consider** the points suggested as a way to come to a deeper understanding of God's word.

■ **Reflect** on and share any new understandings.

■ **Decide** as a family how you will try to live God's word.

■ In this first grade text, some lines from the beautiful Gospel of Luke will be suggested for family faith sharing, prayer, and reflection.

Learn by heart Faith Summary

- We help one another learn about God's love.
- We share our Catholic faith.

A Family Prayer
Pray this prayer with your family.

† Dear God, help us this year to come closer to You. Amen.

Review

When you and your child have worked together on the *Faith Summary* and any of these family activities, invite your child to choose a sticker and place it at the top of the *Faith Alive* page. Do this for every *Faith Alive* page that follows.

Make a Faith Alive Keeper

You need a sheet of cardboard or heavy paper, larger and twice as wide as this page. Fold it in half. Then fold the bottom ends in about 3 inches to make flaps. Tape the flaps. Put your *Faith Alive* pages in your Keeper.

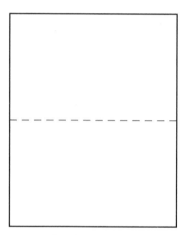

1 Take sheet of paper

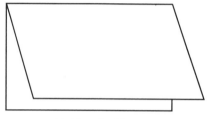

2 Fold in half

3 Fold over sides

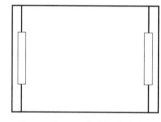

4 Tape down folded sides

5 Write "Faith Alive Keeper" on front

FAMILY SCRIPTURE MOMENT

Gather and **Listen** as the very first words of Luke's Gospel are read expressively.

Dear Theophilus: Many people have done their best to write a report of the things that have taken place among us [concerning Jesus of Nazareth]. They wrote what we have been told by those who saw these things from the beginning and who proclaimed the message. Because I have carefully studied all these matters from their beginning, I thought it would be good to write an orderly account for you. I do this so that you will know the full truth about everything which you have been taught.

From Luke 1:1–4

Share What is Luke saying to us here?

Consider for family enrichment:

■ Luke's Gospel is addressed to Theophilus ("friend or lover of God") and to us. It assures us that God's promises have been fulfilled in Jesus.

■ Luke assures his readers that his message is true and is based on eyewitness accounts. He invites us to deepen our faith in Jesus.

Reflect and **Decide** After rereading Luke 1:1–4, share your hopes in exploring Luke's Gospel together. Pray for hearts and minds open to the good news of Jesus.

In this lesson your child was reminded that God created the world. When was the last time you and your family took time to feel the wonder and beauty of God's creation in a sunrise or sunset, in a walk through a park, in a rainbow, or in the trusting grasp of your child's hand?

You might ask yourself:

■ *When am I most likely to appreciate God's creation? least likely?*

■ *What will I do this week to help my family experience the wonder of God's creation?*

Talk to your child about the beauty of God's world. Then complete these activities together.

Faith Summary
Learn by heart

- God made everything.
- All God's creation is good.

Make a Mobile

Trace the moon
and as many stars as you want.

Color them yellow. Cut them out.
Punch a hole in each one.

Tie them to a clothes hanger with string
of different lengths.

Hang your mobile where the air
will make it move. It will remind you to
thank God for the moon and the stars.

Review

First go over the *Faith Summary* with your child. Then have him or her complete the *Review*. The answers for questions 1–4 appear on the inside back cover. The response to number 5 will help you and your child think about how much she or he has grown to appreciate God's creation. Invite your child to place a sticker on this page.

Circle the correct answer.

1. God made everything good.   Yes   No

2. God's world is ugly.   Yes   No

3. People made the animals.   Yes   No

4. Creation is everything made by God.   Yes   No

5. How will I thank God for all creation?

_____

_____

FAMILY SCRIPTURE MOMENT

As you **Gather** ask your family what each one thinks is the most important thing in life. Now **Listen:**

Look how the wild flowers grow: they don't work or make clothes for themselves. But I tell you that not even King Solomon with all his wealth had clothes as beautiful as one of these flowers. It is God who clothes the wild grass—grass that is here today and gone tomorrow, burned up in the oven. Won't God be all the more sure to clothe you? What little faith you have!

From Luke 12:27–28

Share What is Jesus trying to teach us here?

Consider for family enrichment:

■ Luke's Gospel contains many sayings and parables of Jesus about being dependent on God rather than only on material things for our happiness.

■ Jesus insists that because God cares for all creation, how much more we, the pinnacle of God's creative love, can put our trust in God.

Reflect and **Decide** How do these words of Jesus challenge me to grow in my faith now? What will we do this week as a family to show that we place our trust in God?

Each person is created with unique gifts and must be respected and loved for the way he or she is, not for what we may wish that person to be. Your child especially needs to know that he or she is special to you. Tell your child this week: "In all the world there is no other child like you. We love you because you are you!"

You might ask yourself:

■ *How many people— especially my family— remind me that God made us to be like God?*

■ *Do I remind myself that God does not expect me to be the "perfect parent," but rather one who can forgive myself and others?*

Talk to your child about how wonderful she or he is, and how much God and you love her or him. Then have your child complete the activity below.

Family Photo Album

Show your child some photos of people who are part of your family's life. Talk about what they do, and what makes each one special. Then say this prayer together:

† Thank You, God, for making people.
Thank You, God, for making me so wonderful.
Thank You, God, for making me like You!

Faith Summary
Learn by heart

- God made me wonderful.
- I can know, love, and make things.

Trace the puzzle pieces.
Glue them on heavy paper.
Put the puzzle together.
It will tell you something about yourself.

I AM wonderfully made.

First go over the *Faith Summary* with your child. Then have her or him complete the *Review*. The answers for questions 1–4 appear on the inside back cover. The response to number 5 will help you see whether your child understands how much

God loves him or her. When the *Review* is completed, invite your child to place a sticker on this page.

sticker

Circle the correct answer.

1. God loves you.

Yes   No

2. A teddy bear can know things.

Yes   No

3. God made people.

Yes   No

4. A teddy bear can make things.

Yes   No

5. How does it feel to know that God loves you?

_____

_____

FAMILY SCRIPTURE MOMENT

Before you **Gather** and **Listen** to the words of Jesus, darken the room. Place a bowl over a small lighted lamp or a flashlight. Ask: What happens? Then read what Jesus said about the light of faith.

No one lights a lamp and covers it with a bowl or puts it under a bed. Instead, that person puts it on the lamp stand, so that people will see the light as they come in.

From Luke 8:16

Share How do people in our family or our parish sometimes hide their light of faith?

Consider for family enrichment:
■ In the time of Jesus, small clay lamps filled with oil provided the only light in a house. Keeping the lamp lit was an important daily task.

■ Jesus expects us, who have heard the word of God, to let our faith shine forth. In this way others can see and be guided by the light of our faith.

Reflect Together reread the words of Jesus aloud. Invite each person to light a candle and name one way he or she will let the light of our faith shine for others.

Decide How can we be lights for those in our parish whose faith may be "burning low"?

Life itself is God's first gift to us, a gift that unfolds day by day as we journey in faith as a family. Life is also a call from God to seek the peace of Christ that comes from working for God's reign, or kingdom.

God shares divine life and love with us as the gift of grace. Grace enables us to say, "I am a child of God."

You might ask yourself:

■ *Who or what in our lives and in our society keeps my family and myself from responding fully to God's life?*

■ *What can I do this week to help my child respond each day to God's life in us?*

Have your child complete the activity below. Then talk about how wonderful it is to be a child of God.

Thank God for Life

Talk about your child's birth or adoption. Share how wonderful it is for your family to watch your child grow.

You might want to pray this prayer together.

† Thank You, God, for the gift of (*child's name*).

Faith Summary

Learn by heart

- God gives us the gift of human life.
- Grace is God's own life and love in us.

Paste a picture of yourself in the flower to show you are God's child.

sticker

Circle the correct answer.

1. Human life is precious to God.   (Yes)   No

2. Grace is God's life and love in us.   (Yes)   No

3. A flower can hop.   Yes   (No)

4. I have the gift of human life.   (Yes)   No

5. Why am I happy to be God's child?

_____

_____

_____

 **FAMILY SCRIPTURE MOMENT**

Gather and **Listen** to God's word.

When Joseph and Mary had finished doing all that was required by the law of the Lord, they returned to their hometown of Nazareth in Galilee. The child Jesus grew and became strong; He was full of wisdom, and God's blessings were upon Him.
From Luke 2:39–40

Share How have we as individuals grown in wisdom during the past year?

Consider for family enrichment:

■ This reading follows the presentation of Jesus in the Temple by Mary and Joseph. The Law of Moses required Jewish parents to dedicate their firstborn son to God. Mary and Joseph were faithful Jews.
■ We, too, are dedicated to God at Baptism, which makes us children of God. We can grow in wisdom when we work for the reign of God.

Reflect Invite each person to name one way in which he or she hopes to grow in wisdom this week.

Decide Make a family commitment to grow in wisdom together by doing your best to be faithful to these family Scripture moments. Try to get everyone to agree.

This week your child learned that God the Father, God the Son, and God the Holy Spirit are each equally and eternally God. Yet our faith is always in one God, a unity of three in one. Our faith in the Blessed Trinity helps us to know, love, and care for one another as God knows, loves, and cares for us.
You might ask yourself:

■ *How does my conviction that God loves me enrich my faith? my family life?*

■ *What will I do to help my family express God's knowing, loving, and caring this week?*

Talk About Caring

Have your child show you pictures of people caring for one another. Ask how each is caring for someone. Mention that it is great to have people love you and care for you, but it is even greater to love others and care for them. Talk with your child about ways she or he will care for someone this week. Emphasize our special Christian responsibility to care for the poor.

Conclude by having your child pray this prayer of the Church after you:

† Glory to the Father, and to the Son, and to the Holy Spirit. As it was in the beginning, is now, and will be for ever. Amen.

Faith Summary
Learn by heart

• God knows and loves us.
• God made us to love one another.

Pray the Sign of the Cross with your family.

† In the name of the Father

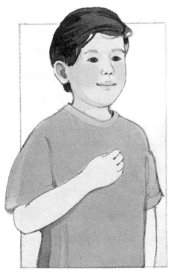

and of the Son

and of the Holy

Spirit.

Amen.

Review

First go over the *Faith Summary* with your child. Then have her or him complete the *Review*. The answers for questions 1–4 appear on the inside back cover. The response to number 5 will help you and your child talk about caring for God's world even at a young age. When the *Review* is completed, invite your child to place a sticker on this page.

Circle the correct answer.

1. We are God's children.   Yes   No

2. There is only one God.   Yes   No

3. God does not know me.   Yes   No

4. There are three Persons in one God.   Yes   No

5. Tell how you will care for our world.

_____

_____

FAMILY SCRIPTURE MOMENT

As a family **Gather** and **Listen** to Luke's account of Jesus' baptism.

After all the people had been baptized, Jesus also was baptized. While He was praying, heaven was opened, and the Holy Spirit came down upon Him in bodily form like a dove. And a voice came from heaven, "You are my own dear Son. I am well pleased with You."
From Luke 3:21–22

Share Invite all to close their eyes and imagine that you are present at the baptism of Jesus. What will you say to Jesus? How will we follow Jesus' example of obedience?

Consider for family enrichment:

■ Jesus was baptized in the Jordan River by John the Baptist. John's baptism was not the sacrament of Baptism as we know it today. But it was a great event that marked the beginning of Jesus' public ministry, when He was affirmed by God and anointed by the Holy Spirit.

■ Soon after His baptism Jesus, the Son of God, began His work of proclaiming the kingdom, or reign of God.

Reflect and **Decide** Recall an experience of Baptism. Ask: What are our hopes for the one being baptized? What are our hopes for ourselves?

This week your child learned the biblical story of the creation of the first human beings. This story is not intended as a literal account of a historical event; it tells us, however, that God is our creator and that human beings lost the original gift of God's friendship because of sin.

God did not abandon the human race. God promised to send a Savior: "The Lord will give you a sign: a young woman is with child and will have a son whom she will call 'Immanuel'" (from Isaiah 7:14). Immanuel means "God is with us."

You might ask yourself:

■ *How has my faith enabled me to be a promise-keeping person, especially to my family?*

■ *This week how will our family show that we are grateful for God's faithful love?*

Use the activity below to talk with your child about the meaning of God's promise.

Keeping Promises

Spend some time talking together about times when your child finds it hard to keep a promise.

Learn by heart **Faith Summary**

- People turned away from God.
- God promised to save us and gave us Jesus, God's own Son.

Spread your arms wide like the rainbow. Say thank you for God's promise.

I will love you always.

From Jeremiah 31:3

Review

First go over the *Faith Summary* with your child. Then have him or her complete the *Review*. The answers for questions 1–3 appear on the inside back cover. The response to number 4 will help you find out the hurts in your child's life over promises that have been broken. When the *Review* is completed, invite your child to put a sticker on this page.

Circle Yes or No.

1. Adam and Eve turned away from God.   Yes   No

2. God promises to be with us always.   Yes   No

3. God keeps God's promises.   Yes   No

4. How do you feel when someone breaks a promise?

_____

_____

FAMILY SCRIPTURE MOMENT

Gather and **Listen** as a family.

One day when Jesus was praying alone, the disciples came to Him. "Who do the crowds say I am?" He asked them. "Some say that You are John the Baptist," they answered. "Others say that You are Elijah, while others say that one of the prophets of long ago has come back to life." "What about you?" He asked them. "Who do you say I am?" Peter answered, "You are God's Messiah."
From Luke 9:18–20

Share If you were present in this gospel scene, how would you respond to Jesus' question "Who do you say I am?"

Consider for family enrichment:
■ Luke depicts Jesus at prayer before He asks His disciples to express their faith in His true identity. Peter recognized Jesus as the Messiah, the Christ or Anointed One, sent by God to save God's people.
■ All of us must know and be able to answer who Jesus is for us and to proclaim Him as our Lord and Savior.

Reflect and **Decide** Imagine that Jesus is seated with your family right now. Tell Him how you will share your faith in Him with others. What will you say? What will you do? Ask Jesus to help you.

In this lesson your child was introduced to a fuller understanding of the word of God in the Bible. The Bible is the word of God to us written in human language. The Second Vatican Council envisions a day when every Catholic will read, know, understand, and love the Bible. The Council urges us to pray over and meditate on the Bible as a primary source of spiritual growth and wisdom for daily life. If you do not already own a family Bible, you might want to get one now, read it often, and keep it in a place of honor in your home.

You might ask yourself:

■ *What will I do to develop and nourish a love for the Bible in my own life?*

■ *How might I help my child begin to develop a love for God's word in the Bible?*

God's Word at Mass

Remind your child of the responses we give to God's word at Mass. At the end of the first reading the reader says, "The word of the Lord." We answer, "Thanks be to God." After the gospel is read, we hear, "The gospel of the Lord." We answer, "Praise to You, Lord Jesus Christ." Help your child make these responses at Mass.

Learn by heart **Faith Summary**

- The Bible tells about God and God's love for us.
- We listen carefully to God's message.

Here is the most important thing the Bible tells us.
Connect the hearts.

sticker

Write the missing word on each line.

Jesus Christ   listen   love

1. God wants us to _____ to God's word.

2. The Bible tells us about God's _____ for us.

3. The Bible tells us that God's best gift to us is _____

_____.

4. Tell a favorite story from the Bible.

FAMILY SCRIPTURE MOMENT

As a family **Gather** and **Listen** to God's word.

On the Sabbath Jesus went as usual to the synagogue. He stood up to read the Scriptures and was handed the book of the prophet Isaiah. He unrolled the scroll and found the place where it was written,

"The Spirit of the Lord is upon me,
because he has chosen me to bring
good news to the poor.
He has sent me to proclaim
liberty to the captives
and recovery of sight to the blind,
to set free the oppressed."

From Luke 4:16–18

Share What is Jesus saying to us in this passage? How do I respond?

Consider for family enrichment:
■ Note that Jesus looked for this text from Isaiah. It was the promise of the great jubilee year to benefit the poor and oppressed, to bring peace and justice for all.
■ This work of justice and peace is at the center of Jesus' ministry. As disciples, we must follow Jesus' example.

Reflect and **Decide** How will we as a family hear the word of God and reach out to those most in need?

In this lesson your child developed a deeper appreciation of what it means to be a saint. As Catholic Christians we use the word saint to refer to those whose lives have been recognized by the Church as "holy or blessed." Saint Paul also used the word to include all those who have done and are doing God's will in their lives. A saint, then, is someone who truly lives the gospel teachings of Jesus Christ. The Second Vatican Council reminds us that all Christians are called by Baptism to such holiness of life.

On November 1, the Church celebrates the feast of All Saints, rejoicing in the holy lives of the countless but unknown saints throughout history. You might ask yourself:

■ *How does the Church's teaching about saints encourage me to live a holy life?*

■ *How might our family celebrate All Saints this year?*

Some Saints I Know

Your child has made some "saints' cards." Let your child share them with you and talk about each one. If possible, find out what you can about the saint for whom you named your child and tell the story to your child.

Learn by heart Faith Summary

- Saints are people who loved God and did God's will on earth.
- We celebrate the feast of All Saints on November 1.

Me—a Saint!

Tell God how you try to be like the saints. Draw a picture to show one way you will do this.

Review

First go over the *Faith Summary* together. Then have your child complete the *Review*. The answers to questions 1–3 appear on the inside back cover. The response to number 4 will help you see whether your child truly understands what it means to be a saint. When the *Review* is completed, have your child choose a sticker to place at the top of the page.

sticker

Circle the correct word.

1. On November 1 we celebrate the feast of

_____.

Thanksgiving   All Saints   Christmas

2. _____ are people who lived as Jesus taught.

Saints   Everyone

3. Saints are now happy with God in

_____.

the Bible   heaven   my parish

4. Tell one thing you can do to live as Jesus taught.

FAMILY SCRIPTURE MOMENT

Gather and **Listen** to Jesus' amazing words:

Do not be afraid, little flock, for your Father is pleased to give you the kingdom. Sell all your belongings and give the money to the poor. Provide for yourselves purses that don't wear out, and save your riches in heaven, where they will never decrease, because no thief can get to them, and no moth can destroy them. For your heart will always be where your riches are.
From Luke 12:32–34

Share How do we feel about this advice from Jesus? Why do we feel that way?

Consider for family enrichment:
■ Jesus insists that His disciples trust in God rather than in material possessions. We must share with others and have a special care for the poor.
■ When our hearts are truly set on doing God's will, we need never be afraid.

Reflect Reread the words of Jesus. Ask: Where are our hearts right now? Name someone you know who is taking these words of Jesus to heart.

Decide How will we as a family or with other parishioners sell something we have and give to the poor?

Trying to cope with bills, sickness, or family difficulties, you might have thought: Jesus never had problems like these. If you have thought this, you were wrong. We know from the Scriptures and the teaching of the Church that Jesus Christ, the Son of God, was one of us and shared our human condition. He was like us in all things but sin. This affirmation of the full humanity as well as the full divinity of Jesus Christ is a central dogma of our faith.

Jesus was born into a human family. We call Jesus, Mary, and Joseph the "Holy Family." Being a holy family does not mean that they did not share experiences familiar to us. The gospel records that Jesus Himself had to grow in "wisdom, age, and grace."

You might ask yourself:

■ *How can reflecting on the Holy Family help our family to grow in "wisdom, age, and grace"?*

■ *What action can we take this week to begin to make this happen?*

Use the activity below to talk with your child about how we can live as Jesus wants.

A Family Prayer

Here is a prayer you can pray with your family.

† Dear Jesus,
Help us to be a loving family.
Help us to be patient and kind.
Help us to reach out to those in need.
Thank You for being with us always.

Happy Feet

Color the music notes that tell ways you can help your family. On the line, write what you will do this week.

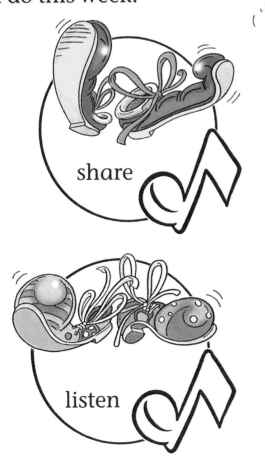

share

listen

pray

Learn by heart Faith Summary

- Jesus is the Son of God.
- Jesus is one of us.

First go over the *Faith Summary* together. Then have your child complete the *Review*. The answers for questions 1–3 appear on the inside back cover. The response to number 4 will help you see how close to Jesus your child feels. When the Review is completed, have your child choose a sticker to place on this page.

Write the missing word on each line.

Christmas   Jesus   Mary

1. **J**_____ is the Son of God.

2. We celebrate Jesus' birth at **C**_____.

3. God chose **M**_____ to be Jesus' Mother.

4. Tell how Jesus is your friend.

_____

_____

FAMILY SCRIPTURE MOMENT

Gather and **Listen** to the angel Gabriel's message to Mary as told by Luke: "Don't be afraid, Mary; God has been gracious to you. You will become pregnant and give birth to a son, and you will name Him Jesus. He will be great and will be called the Son of the Most High God. The Lord God will make Him a king, as His ancestor David was, and He will be the king of the descendants of Jacob forever; His kingdom will never end!"
From Luke 1:30–33

Share What do you hear the angel say to Mary?

How well do we respond to God in our lives?

Consider for family enrichment:
■ Jesus is a name that means "God saves us." Jesus is the Son of God and descendant of David, Israel's greatest king. Jesus is divine and human.
■ God chose Mary, a young woman without power, authority, or influence, to be the mother of Jesus. Her yes to God required great faith, trust, courage, and love.

Reflect and **Decide** What will we do this week to show that we are disciples of Jesus and give our yes to God, as Mary did? Seek Mary's help to follow Jesus by praying a Hail Mary together.

In this lesson your child learned that Jesus Christ is God's best gift to us. Jesus, the second Person of the Blessed Trinity, came into the world to fulfill God's plan of salvation. He showed us who we truly are and who our God is. Out of faithfulness to God, Jesus gave His life and rose again. Through His death and resurrection Jesus Christ brought new life to all humankind.

You might ask yourself:

■ *How does my faith in Jesus help me to be a life-giver in my family?*

■ *How will our family follow the way of Jesus Christ, the Son of God, this week?*

Share your thoughts about Jesus with your child. Then do the following activity together.

Faith Summary
Learn by heart

- Jesus is God's greatest gift to us.
- Jesus shows us He is God's own Son.

Find the missing word.
Paint all the spaces with an **x**.
Then print the word in these sentences.

Jesus is the Son of _____ .

Jesus shows us what _____ is like.

Review

First go over the *Faith Summary* together. Then have your child complete the *Review*. The answers for questions 1–3 appear on the inside back cover. The response to number 4 will help you see whether your child understands what it means to be a friend of Jesus. When the *Review* is completed, have your child choose a sticker for this page.

Write the missing word on each line.

love   Jesus   Son

1. Jesus is God's own **S** _____ .

2. Jesus shows us God's **l** _____ .

3. **J** _____ shows us what God is like.

4. What will you do to show your love for Jesus?

_____

_____

_____

 **FAMILY SCRIPTURE MOMENT**

As a family **Gather** and **Listen** to a story about Jesus.

At daybreak Jesus left the town and went off to a lonely place. The people started looking for Him, and when they found Him, they tried to keep Him from leaving. But He said to them, "I must preach the good news of the kingdom of God in other towns also, because that is what God sent Me to do." So He preached in the synagogues throughout the country.
From Luke 4:42–44

Share What do you think Jesus meant by the kingdom of God? How does He want us to respond to His preaching?

Consider for family enrichment:
■ By "kingdom of God" Jesus meant both God's saving work for all humanity and our response of doing God's will, especially by living with love, justice, and peace.
■ By our Baptism we are called to share our faith with others and to preach the kingdom by our example of our lives.

Reflect and **Decide** How can we grow in living for the kingdom of God this week? Pray the Lord's Prayer as a family.

In this lesson your child met Jesus as *healer*. Jesus befriended all kinds of people. They didn't have to be "religious" or "respectable." Jesus affirmed goodness in people from every walk of life. That is being a healer! One of the surest signs of Jesus' work of salvation was His healing touch. (Salvation comes from a word meaning "health.") He gave sight to the blind and hearing to the deaf, both in the literal and in the spiritual sense.

Most importantly, Jesus offered the healing touch of forgiveness of sins. Again and again He says, as He did to the paralyzed man, "Your sins are forgiven, my friend" (Luke 5:20). We experience the help and healing of Jesus today in the sacrament of Reconciliation, in the Eucharist, in the Christian community, in works of charity and justice, and in prayer.

You might ask yourself:

■ *How do we reflect Jesus as healer in our family?*

■ *How will we try to be more "healing" with one another?*

Prayer Corner

If possible, help your child to set up a prayer corner in his or her room. Place the Bible and pictures of Jesus and the Holy Family in the corner. Reserve a special time in the day when you and your child will go to this corner to pray.

Pray,

✝ Thank You, God, for giving us Jesus as our best friend. Amen.

Think of people who need Jesus' healing love.
Write each person's name on one of the sun's rays.
Ask Jesus to be with him or her.

Learn by heart   Faith Summary

- Jesus cares for all people.
- We can pray to Jesus our friend.

Jesus, send your healing love.

Review
First go over the *Faith Summary* together. Then have your child complete the *Review*. The answers for questions 1–3 appear on the inside back cover. The response to number 4 will help you to find out whether your child needs more

encouragement to talk to Jesus frequently. When the *Review* is completed, have your child choose a sticker for this page.

sticker

Write the missing word on each line.

healed   friend   pray

1. Jesus **h**_____ sick people.

2. We can always talk or **p**_____ to Jesus.

3. Jesus is my **f**_____ .

4. When do you like to pray?

_____

_____

FAMILY SCRIPTURE MOMENT

Gather and **Listen** to God's word.

Once Jesus was in a town where there was a man who was suffering from a dreaded skin disease. When he saw Jesus, he threw himself down and begged Him, "Sir, if You want to, You can make me clean!" Jesus reached out and touched him. "I do want to," He answered. "Be clean." At once the disease left the man.
From Luke 5:12–13

Share Do we turn to Jesus when we are sick and in pain? Why or why not? What do we expect of Him?

Consider for family enrichment:
■ Jesus healed many people as a way of drawing attention to the kingdom of God and as a sign that the Spirit of the Lord was upon Him.
■ One amazing feature of this story is that Jesus *touches* the leper, an act unheard of in Jesus' time.

Reflect Ask: Who are the "lepers" in our society? How are we to reach out to them?

Decide As a family, choose a sick person to whom you will show care this week.

In this lesson your child learned the great Law of Love. Jesus taught God's law that we must love God above all things and we must love others as we love ourselves.

Your child has also learned to pray the Our Father, the prayer that Jesus Himself taught. Help your child pray the Our Father often. It is a reminder of our need to love God above all and to love others as we love ourselves. The *Catechism of the Catholic Church* reminds us that the Lord's Prayer is a summary of the whole gospel.

You might ask yourself:

■ *When will we pray the Our Father together as a family?*

■ *How can our family show that we love others as we love ourselves?*

The Our Father

Slowly pray the Our Father with your child. Then talk about each phrase to help your child to understand its meaning.

Learn by heart

Faith Summary

- God is like a loving parent.
- Jesus taught us the Law of Love.

Pray these words lovingly as you color the ribbon.

Our Father
who art in heaven
hallowed be Thy name.

Review
First go over the *Faith Summary* together. Then
have your child complete the *Review*. The answers
for questions 1–3 appear on the inside back cover.
Pay special attention to your child's response to
number 4. Talk about times when "friends" might
encourage us not to be loving
people as God wants. When
the *Review* is completed, have
your child choose a sticker for
this page.

sticker

Write the missing word on each line.

Our Father   parent   love

1. God is like a loving **p**_____.

2. Jesus taught us the **O**_____ **F**_____.

3. We must **l**_____ God, ourselves, and others.

4. Who teaches you to love God?

_____

_____

FAMILY SCRIPTURE MOMENT

Gather and **Listen** as Jesus
speaks to us:

Ask, and you will receive; seek, and you will find;
knock, and the door will be opened to you. For
everyone who asks will receive, and the one who
seeks will find, and the door will be opened to
anyone who knocks.
From Luke 11:9–10

Share Invite family members to mime or act out
what Jesus is advising us to do. Then ask: What is
your understanding of His message for your life
today?

Consider for family enrichment:

■ Luke's Gospel has many stories and sayings of
Jesus teaching His disciples how to pray. Jesus
encourages us to persevere in prayer, seeking
God's blessing for ourselves and others.

■ God always responds to our prayers, although
not always as we expect.

Reflect and **Decide** For what cause or person
might we as a family ask, seek, and knock? What
will be the special intention of our family prayer
this week?

FAITH ALIVE AT HOME AND IN THE PARISH

In this lesson your child learned about the Last Supper (Holy Thursday), the crucifixion and the burial of Jesus (Good Friday), and His resurrection (Easter Sunday). This period from Holy Thursday evening to Easter Sunday evening is called the Easter Triduum. It is the high point of the Church's liturgical year. As you share the sacred events of the Triduum with your child, remember his or her age. As our children grow, they will share more deeply in the mystery of these days.

You might ask yourself:

■ *What will I do to become more aware of the presence of Jesus in my life? in my family's life?*

■ *How can I share my experience of Jesus in Holy Communion with my child?*

Gifts for Mass

Make a chart, like the one shown, for your kitchen. Ask each family member to draw a picture or a symbol for a gift of a good deed that each will give to Jesus at Mass next week. Some of the symbols shown below may be used.

Then talk with your child about the great love Jesus showed by giving His life for each of us. Say this prayer with your child:

✝ Thank You, Jesus, for giving us Yourself and for promising to help us always. Help us to give ourselves to others, especially to people in need.

Faith Summary

- Jesus gives us the gift of Himself in Holy Communion.
- Jesus died and rose from the dead.

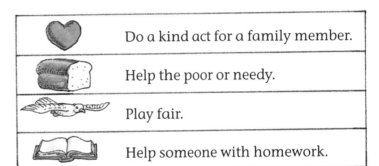

♥	Do a kind act for a family member.
🍞	Help the poor or needy.
	Play fair.
📖	Help someone with homework.

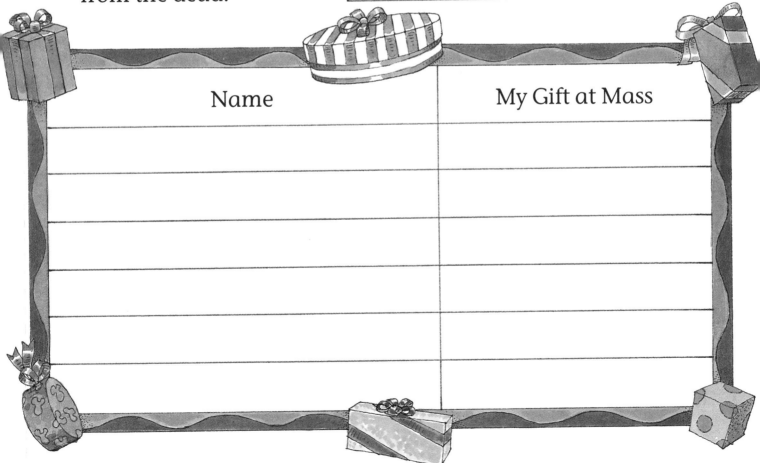

Name	My Gift at Mass

Review

First go over the *Faith Summary* with your child. Then have him or her complete the *Review*. The answers for questions 1–3 appear on the inside back cover. Note the response to number 4 and help your child to follow through on his or her

promise to Jesus. When the *Review* is completed, have your child choose a sticker for this page.

Write the missing word on each line.

died   Jesus   Last Supper

1. Jesus gave us Himself at the L_____

S_____.

2. Holy Communion is the Body and Blood of

J_____.

3. Jesus d_____ for me.

4. What kind thing will I do to bring as a gift to Jesus?

FAMILY SCRIPTURE MOMENT

Gather and **Listen** to what happened when the risen Christ shared a meal with two disciples on the road to Emmaus.

Jesus sat down to eat with them, took the bread, and said the blessing; then He broke the bread and gave it to them. Then their eyes were opened and they recognized Him, but He disappeared from their sight. They said to each other, "Wasn't it like a fire burning in us when He talked to us on the road and explained the Scriptures to us?"

From Luke 24:30–32

Share How or when do we meet Jesus in our lives each day? Do we recognize Him? Why or why not?

Consider for family enrichment:
■ It was only in the breaking of the bread, the sign that Jesus had asked us to do in His memory, that these disciples recognized Him.
■ Do we recognize Jesus in each person we meet, as well as in the Eucharist?

Reflect and **Decide** If possible, read the entire story in Luke 24:13–35. Where will we look for the presence of Jesus this week? Is there someone for whom we will be a sign of the presence of the risen Christ?

In this lesson your child was introduced to the liturgical season of Advent as a time of waiting and preparing. For Catholic Christians, Advent has a dual purpose. It is a time to prepare for Christmas, when we recall and celebrate the first coming of God's Son. It is also a time to turn our minds to Christ's second coming, at the end of time. Advent, then, is a season of joyful and spiritual hope and of expectation for the "day of the Lord."

You might ask yourself:

■ *How does Advent challenge you to "prepare your heart"?*

■ *How can you help your family to prepare thoughtfully and prayerfully for Christmas?*

Learn by heart

Faith Summary

- Advent is a time of waiting to celebrate Jesus' birth at Christmas.
- We prepare for Christmas by praying and helping others.

Share the Advent song with your family and friends.

An Advent Song

(To the tune of "Twinkle, Twinkle Little Star")

Jesus, Jesus, be our light.
Come to make the darkness bright.
Jesus, come and guide our way,
Help us care and love each day.
Jesus, Jesus, be our light.
Come to make the darkness bright.

Review

Go over the *Faith Summary* together before having your child do the *Review*. The answers for questions 1–3 appear on the inside back cover. The response to number 4 will help you to know your child is preparing for Christmas. When the *Review* is completed, have your child choose a sticker for this page.

Circle Yes or No.

1. God promised to send God's Son to us.   Yes   No

2. We celebrate Jesus' birth at Easter.   Yes   No

3. During Advent we get ready for Jesus' birth at Christmas.   Yes   No

4. Tell something you will do to get ready to celebrate Jesus' birth.

_____

_____

_____

FAMILY SCRIPTURE MOMENT

Gather and **Listen** as a family.

Jesus said to the people, "When you see a cloud coming up in the west, at once you say that it is going to rain—and it does. And when you feel the south wind blowing, you say that it is going to get hot—and it does. Hypocrites! You can look at the earth and the sky and predict the weather; why, then, don't you know the meaning of this present time?"
From Luke 12:54–56

Share What signs can we detect that the season of Advent is here?

What is the meaning of this time for our family?

Consider for family enrichment:

■ Christians believe that Jesus will come again at the end of time to usher in the completion of the kingdom of God.

■ Jesus wants us to be alert for His final coming and ready for our own death.

Reflect What might Jesus be asking of our family through this reading from Luke?

Decide What special faith activity will we do as a family this Advent?

In this lesson your child was drawn into the Christmas story through music, prayer, and drama.

The birth of Jesus is not simply a historical event. It is a spiritual reality. Saint Francis of Assisi tells us that Jesus is, in a spiritual way, "born in each of us." Jesus lives in us through the good works we do and the Christian life we live. We are to make God present in our lives every day. In this sense the incarnation continues throughout history.

During the Christmas season, the Church celebrates the incarnation of the Son of God. The Church also celebrates the "epiphanies," or manifestations, of Christ to the magi and again at His baptism by John the Baptist.

You might ask yourself:

■ *How have our family celebrations of Christmas helped us remember that Christ is "born in each of us"?*

■ *How can you help your child to grow in this deeper meaning of Christmas?*

Learn by heart
Faith Summary

- Jesus was born in Bethlehem.
- Jesus wants us to share His love with others.

My Christmas Promise

Sign your name to show Jesus you want to remember this Christmas promise.

Jesus,
I will share Your light and love.

_____

Go over the *Faith Summary* together before having your child complete the *Review.* The answers for questions 1–3 appear on the inside back cover. The response to number 4 will help you see whether your child is growing in the understanding of Christmas. When the *Review* is completed, have your child put a sticker on this page.

Circle Yes or No.

1. There was room for Mary and Joseph at the inn.

Yes   No

2. Angels told shepherds about Jesus' birth.

Yes   No

3. Jesus was born in a stable.

Yes   No

4. Tell how you can share Jesus' love with a friend.

_____

_____

FAMILY SCRIPTURE MOMENT

Gather and share what each one likes about Christmas. Then **Listen** to the Christmas story.

Joseph went from the town of Nazareth in Galilee to the town of Bethlehem in Judea, the birthplace of King David. Joseph went there because he was a descendant of David. He went to register with Mary, who was promised in marriage to him. She was pregnant, and while they were in Bethlehem, the time came for her to have her baby. She gave birth to her first son, wrapped him in cloths and laid him in a manger—there was no room for them to stay in the inn.

Luke 2:4–7

Share What memories does the Christmas story stir up in us? How do we enter into the spirit of Christmas?

Consider for family enrichment:

■ Luke emphasizes that although Jesus was the Son of God, He was born in lowly surroundings.

■ So often Jesus can be "shut out" when the poor and homeless are neglected. To make room for Jesus now means to reach out to people most in need.

Reflect and **Decide** Sing a carol that communicates the Christmas message. Choose one way to serve the poor this Christmas.

My Catholic Faith Book

For the Family

As your child's first grade experience ends, we celebrate with you the ways in which your child has grown as a child of God. You have guided your child's growth in the wisdom of Christian faith, including a love for Scripture. During this year, your child has learned and experienced some very important truths of our faith as they are contained in the *Catechism of the Catholic Church*. For example:

- Creed: God gave us God's Son, Jesus Christ. We are members of God's family, the Church. The Holy Spirit helps us live as children of God.

- Sacraments: We become members of the Church at Baptism. We thank Jesus at Mass for the gift of Himself in the Eucharist. In the sacrament of Reconciliation, we celebrate God's forgiveness. We are strengthened by the Holy Spirit at Confirmation.

- Morality: We try to follow Jesus. We try to love God, one another, and ourselves. We try to be fair and to live in peace.

- Prayer: We listen to God's word in the Bible. We talk to God in our own words. We pray the Our Father, the Hail Mary, and the Sign of the Cross.

Continue to encourage your child to grow in faith by going to Mass together, singing the faith songs, reading Bible stories about God's love for us, and praying together.

Family Prayer

Dear God,
Help our family to continue to grow in faith each day. God, help us as we grow more like Jesus Christ, Your Son. Amen.

This is what we believe…

C God made the world and all people.
Everything God made is good.
God made us and loves us.

R God knows and loves and creates.
God made us to know and love
and make things.

E There is only one God.

E There are three Persons in one God:
God the Father, God the Son, and

D God the Holy Spirit.

We call the three Persons in God
the Blessed Trinity.
God's love for us will never end.

This is how we pray…

P We can pray anywhere or anytime
by ourselves or with others.

R We listen to God's word in the Bible.

A We talk to God in our own words
or say special prayers we have
learned, the Sign of the Cross,
the Our Father, and the Hail Mary.
We begin to learn the Apostles' Creed.

Y We praise God, thank God,
or ask God for help.

E We tell God we are sorry
if we have hurt God

R or other people.

Jesus is God's greatest gift to us. Jesus is God's own Son. He shows us how much God loves us.

Jesus gave us the Law of Love. He told us to love God, others, and ourselves.

Jesus died on Good Friday and rose from the dead on Easter Sunday. He is alive and with us today. Jesus gives us new life.

Jesus gave us the Church.

This is how we live...

M We try to follow Jesus.

O We try to follow the Law of Love.

R We love God, others, and ourselves.

A We care for God's world.

L We care for all people.

I We care especially for the poor and needy.

T We try to live fairly.

Y We try to be peacemakers.

The Church is the community of Jesus' baptized friends.

We are joined together by the Holy Spirit. The Holy Spirit helps the friends of Jesus to be His Church.

We became members of the Church at Baptism. We are Catholic Christians.

At Baptism, we receive God's own life and love. We call this grace.

The Catholic Church is our special home in the Christian family.

The Holy Spirit helps us live as children of God.

We can live forever in heaven with God.

This is how we celebrate...

We celebrate the sacrament of Baptism. When we are baptized, we receive God's own life and love.

In the sacrament of Confirmation we receive the gift of the Holy Spirit in a special way.

We celebrate the Mass. We hear God's word and share the Body and Blood of Christ.

We celebrate the sacrament of Eucharist at Mass. We share Jesus' gift of Himself in Holy Communion.

We celebrate the sacrament of Reconciliation. We tell God we are sorry and we celebrate that God is always ready to forgive us.

S
C
A
R
A
M
E
N
T
S

Of the three Persons of the Blessed Trinity, perhaps the third Person is the least understood and the most neglected in the practice of our faith. The difference that the Spirit can make in our lives becomes abundantly clear when we consider how Pentecost transformed the apostles. After the death of Jesus, the disciples were filled with doubt, fear, and self-recrimination. But when the Holy Spirit came upon them, they were filled with confidence and courage. They proclaimed openly and fearlessly their faith in Jesus.

You might ask yourself:

■ *How often do I speak with my family about ways the Holy Spirit can bring comfort, peace, and happiness?*

■ *How will my family and I turn to the Holy Spirit as our Helper this week?*

Use this activity to talk with your child about ways the friends of Jesus showed their love for one another after they were filled with the Holy Spirit.

Invite your child to talk about times when he or she might need the help of the Holy Spirit. Then say this prayer together:

† Come, Holy Spirit, help us to remember what Jesus said and did. Help us to live as Christians. Help us to tell the good news of Jesus by what we say and by the way we live. Amen.

Learn by heart — Faith Summary

- The Holy Spirit came to the friends of Jesus.
- The Holy Spirit helped the Church to begin and helps us today.

Pray to the Holy Spirit.

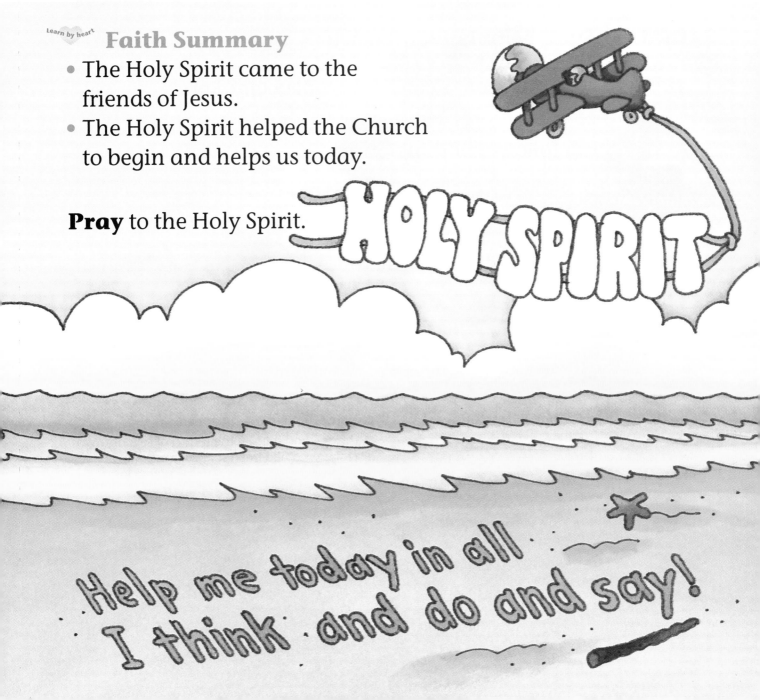

HOLY SPIRIT

Help me today in all I think and do and say!

Review

First go over the *Faith Summary* with your child. Then have him or her complete the *Review*. The answers for questions 1–3 appear on the inside back cover. The response to number 4 will help you discover whether your child understands her or his responsibility as a Christian to help others. When the *Review* is completed, have your child choose a sticker to place on this page.

sticker

Color the circle next to the best answer.

1. The Holy Spirit helps all _____.

○ Christians   ○ animals   ○ plants

2. The Holy Spirit helps Jesus' friends to _____.

○ fight   ○ eat   ○ be peacemakers

3. A _____ is a follower of Jesus Christ.

○ Holy Spirit   ○ Christian   ○ friend

4. Tell how you will help someone today.

FAMILY SCRIPTURE MOMENT

Gather and **Listen** as a family.

At that time Jesus was filled with joy by the Holy Spirit and said, "Father, Lord of heaven and earth! I thank You because You have shown to the unlearned what You have hidden from the wise and learned. Yes, Father, this was how You were pleased to have it happen."

From Luke 10:21

Share Recall times when family members have been filled with joy and enthusiasm by the Holy Spirit. Ask: Why were we joyful? Why do you think Jesus is joyful in this reading?

Consider for family enrichment:

■ This reading follows the return of seventy-two disciples who had been sent on missionary journeys. Jesus rejoices that God's kingdom has been made known through these "everyday people."

■ We do not need special credentials to live the Christian life. But we do need to be open to the guidance and help of the Holy Spirit.

Reflect and **Decide** To what ministries might the Spirit be calling us in our parish? In our family?

This week your child learned how we are to live as Jesus' followers in God's special family, the Church, and how we are to follow the Law of Love. One way to help young children grow as committed members of the Church is to try to provide them with a family life balanced in work, prayer, and play.

Such balance is especially challenging in our culture today. Sometimes families are unhappy because they do not always keep a regular schedule. Children can become confused and upset when they do not eat, sleep, study, and play at the same times each day. Moreover they may become selfish if family members do not model care for one another with definite jobs and responsibilities. Children must be taught the value of working together. This is essential formation for living the Christian life.

You might ask yourself:

■ *How does my family try to live the Law of Love that my child learned about this week?*

It might be fun to create a weekly chart that shows the times for bed, meals, and so on. The chart could also list each person's weekly tasks with room for each one to check when it has been done satisfactorily. Plan a family treat for the weekend after each one has done the weekly tasks well.

Use the activity below to talk with your child about ways Jesus' friends help one another.

Praying Together

Share with your child a prayer of thanks for belonging to the Church. You may wish to use the following prayer:

✝ Jesus, thank You for inviting me to belong to Your Church. Help me and my family to do our part by following Your way.

Learn by heart

Faith Summary

- Jesus invites everyone to belong to His Church.
- We are part of the Church and try to treat others as Jesus did.

As you color each bead, say the prayer to Jesus on the clasp.

Jesus, I am your friend.

First go over the *Faith Summary* with your child. Then have him or her complete the *Review*. The answers for questions 1–3 appear on the inside back cover. The response to number 4 will help you find out whether your child knows how to begin each day with a new promise to follow Jesus. When the *Review* is completed, have your child choose a sticker to place on this page.

Color the circle next to each correct answer.

1. The leader of the whole Church is the _____.

○ bishop   ○ pope   ○ priest

2. We belong to the _____.

○ circus   ○ sea   ○ Church

3. The Church of Jesus is for _____.

○ Paul   ○ everyone   ○ no one

4. How will I be a follower of Jesus this week?

FAMILY SCRIPTURE MOMENT

Gather and **Listen** as Jesus tells us one of His parables about the kingdom of God.

Jesus asked, "What is the kingdom of God like? What shall I compare it with? It is like this. Someone takes a mustard seed and plants it in his field. The plant grows and becomes a tree, and the birds make their nests in its branches."
From Luke 13:18–19

Share what each one hears from this parable for his or her life.

Consider for family enrichment:

■ Jesus frequently told stories and parables about the kingdom of God. It was His central message. Like the mustard tree, the kingdom is to grow so that all people can make their home within its welcoming branches.

■ We help the kingdom grow when we "water" it with prayer, worship, and works of justice, peace, and mercy.

Reflect Reread the parable. Ask: What do we hear for our lives now?

Decide Choose something to do as a family this week to bring about the kingdom in our family and in our parish.

Memories are very important to a child. Telling your child the story of her or his own Baptism, especially your family's joy on that day, will help your child feel happy about being a child of God.

The next time you take your child to church, point out the place of Baptism (immersion pool or font). Explain how each of us as baptized persons has the responsibility to live each day as a follower of Jesus and to carry on His work. This does not mean doing only extraordinary things, but rather the small, everyday things as best we can. It means caring especially for those in need and those who are treated unjustly. Your example in living out your own baptismal witness will help your child in living the Catholic Christian faith.

You might ask yourself:

■ *What does Baptism mean to me in my daily life?*

Act out with your child his or her Baptism. Then have your child do the activity below.

A Family Prayer

Talk with your child about God's life within us. Teach him or her to reflect quietly on this wonder of God's love. You might like to lead your child in the following reflective prayer.

Close Your Eyes

✝ Think quietly for a few minutes about God's life in you. Then thank God in your own words for this wonderful gift. Ask God to help you share this gift with others.

Learn by heart
Faith Summary

- We share in God's own life when we are baptized.
- Baptism makes us children of God and members of Jesus' Church.

I Am God's Child

How do you grow as God's child? Write your name or put yourself in the flower. Think quietly about God's life in you. Thank God for this wonderful gift.

Review

First go over the *Faith Summary* with your child. Then have him or her complete the *Review*. The answers for questions 1–4 appear on the inside back cover. The response to number 5 will show you whether your child is beginning to understand what it means to live as a child of God. When the *Review* is completed, have your child choose a sticker to place on this page.

Color the circle next to each correct answer.

1. You became God's child at _____.

○ Baptism   ○ born   ○ singing

2. The Church uses _____ to baptize.

○ sand   ○ water   ○ sugar

3. Because we are baptized, we live like _____.

○ plants   ○ birds   ○ Jesus

4. In Baptism we receive God's own _____.

○ cross   ○ life   ○ body

5. What will you do this week to show you are God's child?

FAMILY SCRIPTURE MOMENT

Gather and discuss what you think Jesus' attitude was towards small children. Then **Listen** to this beautiful story about Jesus and the children.

Some people brought their children to Jesus for Him to place His hands on them. The disciples saw this and scolded them for doing so, but Jesus called the children to Him and said, "Let the children come to Me and do not stop them, because the kingdom of God belongs to such as these. Remember this! Whoever does not receive the kingdom of God like a child will never enter it."

From Luke 18:15–17

Share What did we hear in this reading for our lives?

Consider for family enrichment:

■ Belonging to the kingdom of God demands a childlike trust. Adults should not think that they can gain the kingdom simply by effort or brainpower!

■ Childlike does not mean "childish." We are to place our faith and trust in God as children would a loving parent.

Reflect Ask: What does it mean for me to accept the kingdom of God as a child would?

Decide on something to do to celebrate and cherish the child in each family member.

Some children and adults find Mass boring because they do not appreciate what the Eucharist celebration means. All that we are and do as Catholics should lead to and flow from the liturgy. Each of the other sacraments is connected to and directed toward the Eucharist. All Catholic Christians should be able to find in the weekly liturgy a source of nurture in Christian living.

We can strengthen our family's appreciation of the Mass by good preparation. For example:

■ explaining what will happen at Mass;

■ reading and reflecting on the readings for the liturgy;

■ asking each family member to do one good deed each day as a special gift to bring to Jesus at Mass.

Ask your child what good deed she or he would like to bring to Jesus at Mass this week. Talk about it together. Then have your child complete the activity below.

Mass Booklet

On pages of your child's religion book, you will find *My Mass Book*. Help your child make this booklet and encourage him or her to use it at Mass.

Faith Summary
Learn by heart

- Jesus is with us each time we celebrate the Mass.
- We all have a part to play in the Mass.

Draw the gift you will bring to Jesus.

Review

First go over the *Faith Summary* with your child. Then have him or her complete the *Review.* The answers for questions 1–3 appear on the inside back cover. The response to number 4 will help you find out whether your child is growing in her or his knowledge and love for the Mass. When the *Review* is completed, have your child place a sticker on this page.

sticker

Color the circle next to each correct answer.

1. Jesus is with us each time we celebrate _____.

○ the Mass ○ breakfast ○ hockey

2. The special Mass table is the _____.

○ altar ○ candle ○ cross

3. Our leader at Mass is the _____.

○ teacher ○ priest ○ me

4. Tell about your favorite way of taking part in the Mass.

FAMILY SCRIPTURE MOMENT

Gather and **Listen** as Jesus speaks to us:

So watch what you do! If your brother sins, rebuke him, and if he repents, forgive him. If he sins against you seven times in one day, and each time he comes to you saying, "I repent," you must forgive him.

From Luke 17:3–4

Share How do you feel about this challenging teaching of Jesus to forgive always, no matter what?

Consider for family enrichment:

■ In the Bible, the number seven means without limit. There should be no end to our forgiving others.

■ We forgive others because we trust that God forgives us. We pray "forgive us our trespasses…."

Reflect Ask family members to recall in silence one thing for which they have not forgiven others fully, and to imagine what they will do about it.

Decide Pray together for Jesus' healing power of forgiveness. Pray the Lord's Prayer (or Our Father) together and share a sign of peace.

In this lesson your child continues to learn what happens during Mass. The better we parents understand the Mass, the more we can help our children to appreciate it. It is important that we realize that Jesus is truly present to us in the Liturgy of the Word, preparing us for communion with Him in the Liturgy of the Eucharist. Having been reconciled and nourished by the word, we are called to the Lord's Supper in the Liturgy of the Eucharist. Along with the bread and wine, we offer ourselves to God as a living sacrifice of gratitude and praise.

During the Eucharistic Prayer, the bread and wine become the Body and Blood of Christ. This is done through the words and actions of the priest and the power of the Holy Spirit. In Holy Communion, we are united with Jesus Christ and with one another as members of Christ's Body in the world.

Renewed by the Eucharist, we are called to try to be "bread of life" for others—especially the poor, the suffering, and those who have been deprived of life and love.

Mass Booklet

Continue helping your child use the Mass booklet from text pages during Mass.

Learn by heart ## Faith Summary

- We listen to God's word at Mass.
- Our gifts to God become Jesus, whom we receive in Holy Communion.

Lord, hear our prayer.

I Join in the Mass

Draw yourself with the people at Mass. Then say the response prayer.

Color the circle next to each correct answer.

1. The _____ is the good news of Jesus.

○ singing   ○ gospel   ○ loving

2. The prayer that tells what we believe is the

○ Our Father   ○ Creed   ○ Hail Mary

3. At Mass the bread and wine become ____.

○ Mary   ○ Jesus   ○ Paul

4. How will you try to be a peacemaker this week?

FAMILY SCRIPTURE MOMENT

Gather and **Listen** as Jesus tells us about a woman He admires.

Jesus looked around and saw rich men dropping their gifts in the Temple treasury, and He also saw a very poor widow dropping in two little copper coins. He said, "I tell you that this poor widow put in more than all the others. For the others offered their gifts from what they had to spare of their riches; but she, poor as she is, gave all she had to live on."
From Luke 21:1–4

Share Have family members imagine that they are the widow in the story. Ask: To whom would you be so generous? Why?

Consider for family enrichment:
■ Jesus loves the widow because she gives the little she has while trusting that God will provide for her.
■ The widow is a more faith-filled person than the rich people who give from their excess wealth and find their security in material possessions.

Reflect What might our family do this week to respond to Jesus' challenge in this story?

Decide Pray together: Loving God, give us a generous heart toward those most in need.

In this lesson your child was introduced to the liturgical season of Lent as a special time for prayer and good works. It is a time of preparation for the most important moments of the Church year—the remembrance and celebration of the life, death, and resurrection of Christ. Lent should be a positive experience for your child, not a negative one. It is also a time when we are especially one with those preparing to be initiated into the Church during the Easter Vigil.

The Church encourages us to prepare in a spirit of loving self-sacrifice by praying and studying Scripture, by fasting, by giving alms to the poor, and by ministering to those in need.

You might ask yourself:

■ *What aspect of my life should I review during this Lenten season?*

■ *How can I help my child participate—at an appropriate level—in the family's Lenten observance?*

You can begin by doing this activity with your child.

Learn by heart

Faith Summary

- Lent is a special time to grow in love for Jesus.
- We remember that Jesus died for us and rose from the dead.

A Place to Pray

Finish the picture of a place where Jesus prayed.
Imagine you are with Jesus there.
When you pray during Lent, picture yourself in this place with Jesus.

Review

Go over the *Faith Summary* together. Then have your child complete the *Review.* The answers for questions 1–3 appear on the inside back cover. The response to number 4 will help you find out whether your child has a growing understanding of Lent. When the *Review* is completed, have your child place a sticker on this page.

Write the correct answer.

Lent   love   pray

1. Jesus wants us to grow in His _____Love_____ .

2. ___Len___ is a special time to do this.

3. We ___pray___ to Jesus for help.

4. Tell one way you will try to grow in love.

_____W. W. J. D_____

_____

FAMILY SCRIPTURE MOMENT

Gather and **Listen** as a family.

One of the criminals hanging there hurled insults at Jesus: "Aren't you the Messiah? Save yourself and us!" The other one, however, rebuked him, saying, "Don't you fear God? You received the same sentence He did. Ours, however, is only right, because we are getting what we deserve for what we did; but He has done no wrong." And he said to Jesus, "Remember me, Jesus, when you come as King!" Jesus said to him, "I promise you that today you will be in paradise with Me."

From Luke 23:39–43

Share What do we learn for our own lives from Jesus' forgiveness of the "good thief"?

Consider for family enrichment:

■ The "good thief" wins Jesus' admiration because he trusts totally in God. In faith, the thief recognizes the Son of God and is assured of God's mercy.

■ Lent is a special time for offering and receiving forgiveness.

Reflect and **Decide** Have each person tell the personal lesson learned from this story. How will we renew our confidence in Jesus' forgiveness this week?

FAITH ALIVE AT HOME AND IN THE PARISH

In this lesson your child learned that after Jesus died He rose to new life. It is this new life that He shares with us. We celebrate the resurrection of Jesus every Sunday.

But the high point is Easter Sunday itself. It is the day of Jesus' final victory over death and destruction—it is the feast of our Christian hope. We are assured in the resurrection of Jesus that we, too, can rise with Him to new life.

Easter, then, is a time for a renewed and living faith—a faith that reaches out to the poor, the abandoned, and the homeless, so that they may also find the hope of new life in our acts of Christian love, concern and justice.

You might ask yourself:

■ *How does the Easter message give me hope?*

■ *How can our family bring the hope of Easter to someone else? to people in our parish?*

Learn by heart **Faith Summary**

- Jesus rose from the dead on Easter.
- Jesus gives us new life.

New Life

Celebrate the new life Jesus gives at Easter.
Decorate the T-shirt with signs of Easter joy.

Review
Go over the Faith Summary together before having your child complete the *Review*. The answers for questions 1–3 appear on the inside back cover. Use the response to number 4 to discuss your child's feelings about Jesus' new life. When the *Review* is completed, have your child put a sticker on the page.

sticker

Circle the correct word.

1. Jesus gives us new _____.

   clothes   life

2. We celebrate Jesus' new life on _____.

   Easter   New Year's Day

3. When Jesus' friend went to His tomb, it was _____.

   closed   empty

4. How will you share with someone the good news of Easter?

FAMILY SCRIPTURE MOMENT

Gather and **Listen** to the joyful Easter story.

Very early on Sunday morning the women went to the tomb, carrying the spices they had prepared. They stood there puzzled about this [the empty tomb], when suddenly two men in bright shining clothes stood by them. Full of fear, the women bowed down to the ground, as the men said to them, "Why are you looking among the dead for one who is alive? He is not here; He has been raised. Remember what He said to you while He was in Galilee: 'The Son of Man must be handed over to sinful men, be crucified, and three days later rise to life.'"

From Luke 24:1,4–7

Share Imagine you were at the tomb on the first Easter. How might you have reacted?

Consider for family enrichment:

■ This story of the resurrection shows us the women disciples at the empty tomb. They are the first witnesses to tell of Jesus' resurrection from the dead.

■ The resurrection is the heart of the Christian faith. We, too, go forth to share this joyful message with others.

Reflect and **Decide** How will your family celebrate your Easter faith this year? Think of something very special to do together.

Parishes are joined together in a diocese under the leadership of the bishop. All the bishops, together with the pope as bishop of Rome, serve as leaders of the universal Church.

The parish is our home in the Catholic Church. It is critical that every Catholic feels a sense of welcome and belonging in his or her parish home. Whether or not children will feel that they belong to their Catholic faith as adults will depend very much on their feelings of belonging to their parish as children. You have to build up this sense of parish as home for your family and for your fellow parishioners.

You might ask yourself:

■ *In what ways does my parish welcome me and help me feel I belong? In what ways do I help others feel they belong?*

■ *In what ways can I and my family share in the liturgical and catechetical life of our parish?*

One way to help children feel the parish is their home is to have them invite friends to the parish church. You might want to do the activity below with your child.

A Family Prayer

Pray this prayer for the Church with your child.

† Jesus, bless our parish family.
Bless Your Church all over the world.
Help us to live like You.
Help us to share Your good news with everyone.

Faith Summary

learn by heart

- Our parish is our special place in the Catholic Church.
- Everyone helps in our parish.

Invite a friend to visit your parish church. Practice your invitation here. Then copy it on note paper.

Join Us

FOR: _____

DATE: _____ TIME: _____

PLACE: _____

_____

sticker

Circle the correct word.

1. Our parish has a special building called the parish _____.

church   altar

2. We _____ to God in our parish church.

pray   name

3. The _____ leads us as we worship God at Mass.

priest   team

4. Tell how you feel about belonging to your parish.

FAMILY SCRIPTURE MOMENT

Gather and **Listen** as a family.

An argument broke out among the disciples as to which one of them should be thought of as the greatest. Jesus said to them, "The kings of the pagans have power over their people, and the rulers claim the title 'Friends of the People.' But this is not the way it is with you; rather, the greatest among you must be like the youngest, and the leader must be like the servant. Who is greater, the one who sits down to eat or the one who serves? The one who sits down, of course. But I am among you as one who serves."

From Luke 22:24–27

Share What do we hear Jesus saying in the words, "I am among you as one who serves"? What are some ways we can serve one another?

Consider for family enrichment:

■ Luke places Jesus' teaching about greatness and service in the context of the Last Supper. The disciples of Jesus are not to lord it over others but to lovingly serve others, as He did.

■ As disciples, we are also called to serve others in the Christian community and the world, especially those most in need.

Reflect and **Decide** What does it mean to be great among those who follow Jesus? How will we show greatness in the parish this week?

When we take part often, knowingly, and lovingly in the Church's life of prayer and worship, we experience ourselves as a priestly people. It is an aspect of our baptismal commitment to "proclaim the wonderful acts of God, who called us out of darkness into God's own marvelous light" (from 1 Peter 2:9).

Celebrating the sacraments and praying often as a family are wonderful ways to help our children grow strong in their Christian faith and in their love of God.

You might ask yourself:

■ *What sacraments and other Church celebrations help me most in my daily life?*

■ *When will I take time for personal prayer this week?*

Have your child say the Hail Mary slowly with you. Talk about what it means to both of you.

Reflective Prayer

Before your child goes to bed, you might gently ask one or two questions like these: Did you help anyone today? Did you play fairly? Did you try to do your best work in school? Then together thank God for the times your child did one of these things.

Learn by heart
Faith Summary

- Catholics celebrate the sacraments.
- Catholics pray to God.

Add some of your favorite things to the card.

Hail Mary,
full of grace,
The Lord is with you.

Hello,

_____.
(your name)
I am a child of God.
The Lord is with me.

Pray and **remember.**

Review

First go over the *Faith Summary* with your child. Then have him or her complete the *Review*. The answers for questions 1–3 appear on the inside back cover. The response to number 4 will help you see whether your child feels comfortable with praying and is developing the habit of praying often. When the *Review* is completed, have your child place a sticker on this page.

Circle the correct word.

1. The prayer that Jesus taught us is the _____.

Our Father   Bible

2. To worship is to give honor and praise to _____.

others   God

3. Catholics celebrate the _____.

sacraments   candles

4. What is your favorite prayer?

When do you pray this prayer?

FAMILY SCRIPTURE MOMENT

Gather and tell about some of the "mighty" things God has done for you. Then **Listen** to Mary's song of praise.

My heart praises the Lord;
   my soul is glad because of
      God my Savior,
   for God has remembered me,
      God's lowly servant!
From now on all people will
   call me blessed,
   because of the great things
      the Mighty God has done for me.

Luke 1:46–49

Share For us, what does it mean to be blessed?

Consider for family enrichment:

■ These are the first lines of Mary's canticle, the Magnificat. She shared this song of praise with Elizabeth, expressing her joy in being chosen by God as the mother of God's own Son.

■ Mary's canticle is part of the daily Evening Prayer of the Church. It reminds us that God works through the "little ones" to accomplish great works of love, justice, and peace.

Reflect and **Decide** Pray the Magnificat together. Invite each person to choose one way to be God's faithful servant this week.

The Church's social teaching on justice and peace is soundly rooted in the Old and New Testaments. That the covenant demands justice is a constant theme of the Hebrew prophets.

From the proclamation of Jesus' birth to His farewell at the Last Supper, the life of Christ preaches justice and peace to all people. The Catholic Church clearly teaches that our Christian faith gives us serious social responsibilities. All of us are called to work for God's kingdom of justice and peace in the world.

Children need to be given opportunities to practice fairness and forgiveness in their daily lives. In the family the habits of justice, mercy, and peace must be sown if children are to grow to be just and merciful adults.

You might ask yourself:

■ *How do we as a family respond to the Church's call to be people of justice, mercy, and peace?*

■ *What will we do this week to make the first move toward peace with someone or some group?*

To help your child to be a peaceful person, pray with him or her in the way described below.

Talk About Fairness

Help your child in his or her daily life to notice opportunities for practicing fairness with others. Also encourage your child to talk with Jesus about hurts and worries.

Learn by heart Faith Summary

- Catholics try to treat others fairly and live in peace.
- Jesus wants us to be peacemakers.

Finding Peace

Close your eyes. Breathe in and out slowly. Imagine you are a boat, sailing in the wind. Pray this prayer.

Peace to you.
Peace to me.
Peace within our family.

Review

First go over the *Faith Summary* with your child. Then have him or her complete the *Review*. The answers for questions 1–3 appear on the inside back cover. The response to number 4 will give you the chance to talk about the times when she

or he finds it hard to be fair. When the *Review* is completed, have your child place a sticker on this page.

Circle the correct word.

1. Jesus gave the gift of _____ to us.

   peace   sadness

2. When we are fair to one another, we can live in _____.

   sadness   peace

3. Being fair is treating people the way we _____.

   feel like treating them   want them to treat us

4. I will try to be fair _____.

   sometimes   always

FAMILY SCRIPTURE MOMENT

Gather and **Listen** as Jesus speaks to us.

A healthy tree does not bear bad fruit, nor does a poor tree bear good fruit. Every tree is known by the fruit it bears; you do not pick figs from thorn bushes or gather grapes from bramble bushes. A good person brings good out of the treasure of good things in the heart. For the mouth speaks what the heart is full of.

From Luke 6:43–45

Share What evidence, or "fruit," do we produce to show we are Christians?

Consider for family enrichment:

■ Jesus used the example of a fig tree because figs were an important source of energy and nutrition to the people of His country. Figs were eaten year-round.

■ Our good words and deeds of Christian service must come from our hearts.

Reflect and ask, "What is the good fruit that I want to bring forth as a Christian?"

Decide How will our mouths speak what our hearts are full of to the sick or the needy this week?

In this lesson your child has been given a basic understanding that in the sacrament of Reconciliation the Church continues Jesus' ministry of forgiving sinners. Such forgiveness means not just telling God we are sorry, but also seeking ways of repairing any harm done to those we have hurt. This lesson also helps your child understand the need for each of us to forgive others.

You and your family must also help your child begin to understand what it means to say both "I am sorry" and "I forgive you." This means showing *how* you are sorry and *how* you forgive.

Think of ways you can model both to your child this week.

Talk with your child about how he or she feels when forgiving or when being forgiven. Then ask your child to complete the activity below.

Sharing Prayers

Go over this part of the Our Father with your child:

✝ "Forgive us our trespasses as we forgive those who trespass against us."

Point out the importance of forgiving others as we wish God to forgive us.

Learn by heart Faith Summary

- God always forgives us if we are sorry.
- The Church forgives in God's name.

Circle how you feel when you forgive or when you are forgiven. Act it out.

Circle the correct word.

1. God forgives us when we are _____.

   sorry   happy

2. _____ brings us God's forgiveness.

   John   Jesus

3. God will _____ love us.

   always   sometimes

4. Tell how you feel when you have been forgiven.

FAMILY SCRIPTURE MOMENT

Gather and ask: How important is forgiveness in everyday living? Then **Listen** to the words of Jesus in this story.

Then Jesus said to the woman, "Your sins are forgiven." The others sitting at the table began to say to themselves, "Who is this, who even forgives sins?" But Jesus said to the woman, "Your faith has saved you; go in peace."
Luke 7:48–50

Share Invite family members to share what they heard in this reading.

Consider for family enrichment:
■ This reading is an excerpt from a story about a sinful woman who humbly washed Jesus' feet and anointed His head when He was at the home of Simon the Pharisee. Because she showed such great love for Jesus, He forgave all her sins. We, too, receive God's forgiveness in a special way in the sacrament of Reconciliation.

■ When we forgive others, we reflect the mercy and compassion of God.

Reflect How and for what will we try to show forgiveness in our family?

Decide Exchange some sign of peace and forgiveness with one another.

Your child has now completed *Coming to God,* the first grade book about our Catholic faith. Your family is to be congratulated for its continued interest and support in your child's growth in faith. Your interest need not stop here but should continue through the coming weeks with experiences of prayer and good works. Living as friends of Jesus is a lifetime vocation.

Recall with your child some of the most important truths learned this year. Discuss the importance of God's word and presence in your family's life. You may wish to end by acting out the poem adapted from Ephesians 3:17.

With your child make a weekly chart to show how he or she can live as a child of God.

Remembering Baptism

Discuss with your child God's unending love. Light a candle and pray:

✝ "This is the light of Christ. May it always burn brightly in your heart and lead you to be with God forever and ever."

Wider than the widest sea

Faith Summary

Learn by heart

- Jesus wants us to be with Him forever.
- God's love will never end.

Taller than the tallest tree

Deep as the deepest lake can be—

God's Love for Me

Move your arms to help you remember what God's love is like.

That is God's great love for me!

Review
First go over the *Faith Summary* with your child. Then have him or her complete the *Review*. The answers for questions 1–3 appear on the inside back cover. The response to number 4 will help you motivate your child to remember to keep close to God during the summer. When the *Review* is completed, have your child choose a sticker for this page.

sticker

Circle the correct word.

1. God will stay with me _____.

    a day   forever

2. God's _____ will last forever.

    love   fear

3. Jesus blessed the _____.

    day   children

4. Tell one thing you will do to show you are God's child.

FAMILY SCRIPTURE MOMENT

Gather and ask: What do you think Jesus loves so much about children? Then **Listen** to our final reading from Luke's gospel.

An argument broke out among the disciples as to which one of them was the greatest. Jesus knew what they were thinking, so He took a child, stood the child by His side, and said to them, "Whoever welcomes this child in My name, welcomes Me; and whoever welcomes Me, also welcomes the One who sent Me. For the one who is least among you is the greatest."

From Luke 9:46–49

Share In what ways are we, no matter how old we get, to remain like children?

Consider for family enrichment:

◼ Jesus understands that His disciples will always be tempted to be "big and important," to be "the greatest" in other people's eyes. So He tells them that real greatness is to be childlike before God.

◼ By our Baptism we are God's children, called to welcome and serve, as Jesus did.

Reflect Reread Luke 9:46–49. What will we remember best about this reading?

Decide Close with a simple fun family celebration that includes a prayer of thanksgiving to God.

Morning Offering

My God, I offer you today
all I think and do and say,
uniting it with what was done
on earth, by Jesus Christ,
your Son.

Evening Prayer

Dear God, before I sleep
I want to thank you
for this day so full of
your kindness and your joy.
I close my eyes to rest
safe in your loving care.

My
Prayer
Screen

A Listening Prayer

God, open our ears
and hearts to listen
to your word.

Prayers from the Bible

From Psalm 27:11

God,
teach me to do
what you want.
Please show me
the way.

God,
I am always
in your care.

From Psalm 31:15

Grace Before Meals

Bless us, O Lord,
and these your gifts,
which we are about to receive
from your bounty,
through Christ our Lord.
Amen.

Grace After Meals

We give you thanks,
almighty God,
for these and all your gifts
which we have received
through Christ our Lord.
Amen.

GLUE

FOLD

GLUE

FOLD

Prayer of Quiet

Sit in a comfortable position.
Relax by breathing in and out.
Shut out all the sights
and sounds.
Each time you breathe in
and out, say the name "Jesus."

Prayer for Peace

Give us peace, Jesus,
in our hearts.
Give us peace, Jesus,
in our homes.
Give us peace, Jesus,
with our friends.
Give us peace, Jesus,
in our Church.
O, Jesus, give us peace.

Family Prayer

Come, Holy Spirit,
fill our hearts
with love.

Holy Family,
help our family
to be a
holy family, too.

A Family Blessing

May God bless us and
    take care of us.
May God be kind to us.
May God look on us
    with favor.
May God give us peace,
    every season, every year.

From Numbers 6:24–26

FOLD

GLUE

back of screen 2

GLUE

GLUE

FOLD

Prayers for Church Seasons

Advent

Come, Lord Jesus.

Christmas

Jesus, we welcome you
into our hearts.

Lent

Jesus, help me spend
quiet time with you.

Easter

Alleluia, Jesus!
We have good news
to tell.

Ordinary Time

Jesus, may our friendship
with you keep on growing.

Hail Mary

Hail Mary, full of grace,
the Lord is with you;
blessed are you
among women,
and blessed is the fruit
of your womb, Jesus.
Holy Mary, Mother of God,
pray for us sinners
now and at the hour
of our death.
Amen.

I Believe

I believe in God,
the Father almighty,
creator of heaven and earth.

The rest of the Apostles' Creed
will be taught in Grades 2 and 3.

FOLD

Sign of the Cross

In the name of the Father,
and of the Son,
and of the Holy Spirit.
Amen.

Our Father

Our Father, who art in heaven,
hallowed be thy name;
thy kingdom come;
thy will be done on earth
as it is in heaven.
Give us this day our daily bread
and forgive us our trespasses
as we forgive those
who trespass against us;
and lead us not into temptation
but deliver us from evil.
Amen.

FOLD

Glory to the Father

Glory to the Father,
and to the Son,
and to the Holy Spirit
as it was in the beginning,
is now, and will be for ever.
Amen.

A Vocation Prayer

God, I know you will
call me for special work
in my life. Help me
to follow Jesus each day
and be ready to answer
your call.

We honor Mary, the mother of Jesus, God's own Son.

We use statues and pictures to help us remember:
- Mary cared for Jesus.
- She is our mother, too.

Mary's special month is May.

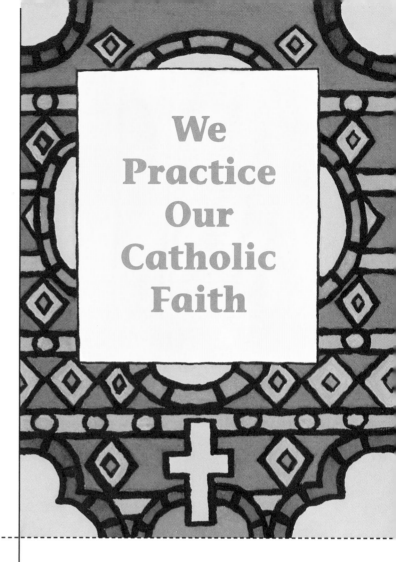

We Practice Our Catholic Faith

Cut on this line.

We pray to God at home by ourselves or with our families.
We pray to God in church with our parish family.

Fold on this line.

We are baptized.
We are God's children.
We use holy water as a sign of our Baptism.

We often begin our prayers to God with the sign of the cross.
Bless yourself by making the sign of the cross with your right hand.

Fold on this line.

We celebrate special days called holy days.

- The Immaculate Conception (December 8)

- Christmas (December 25)

- Mary, Mother of God (January 1)

- Ascension Thursday (40 days after Easter)

- Assumption of Mary (August 15)

- All Saints Day (November 1)

Cut on this line.

Mass is our great celebration together.
We take part in the Mass on Sunday or on Saturday evening.

We show respect and love for God in church.
Genuflect by bending your right knee to the floor.

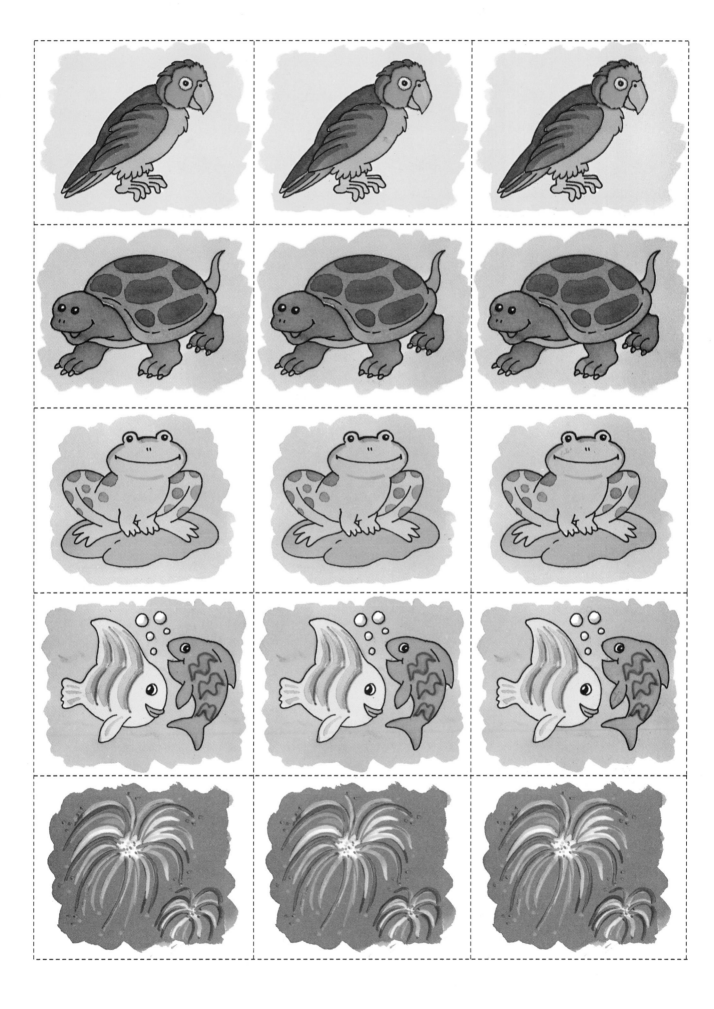